BABY OWL

Published in Canada by Fitzhenry & Whiteside, 195 Allstate Parkway, Markham, Ontario L3R 4T8

Published in the United States by Fitzhenry & Whiteside, 311 Washington, Brighton, Massachusetts 02135

10 9 8 7 6 5 4 3 2

National Library of Canada Cataloguing in Publication Data
Lang, Aubrey
Baby owl / text by Aubrey Lang ; photography by Wayne Lynch
(Nature babies)
ISBN 1-55041-796-7 (bound).—ISBN 1-55041-798-3 (pbk.)
1. Owls—Infancy—Juvenile literature. I. Lynch, Wayne
II.Title.   III. Series: Lang, Aubrey. Nature babies.
QL696.S8L35 2003   j598.9'7   C2002-905293-9

U.S. Cataloging-in-Publication Data
(Library of Congress Standards)
Lang, Aubrey.
Baby owl / text by Aubrey Lang ; photography by Wayne Lynch. — 1st ed.
[36] p. : col. photos. ; cm.   (Nature babies)
Includes bibliographical references and index.
Summary: As their nest becomes more and more crowded, the baby great horned owls stretch and flap impatiently. But they can't fly just yet. Even if one of them falls from the tree and must find its own shelter on the ground, the little one still depends on its parents' care. There are many weeks to go before the young chicks will be strong enough to fly away and find homes of their own.
ISBN 1-55041-796-7   ISBN 1-55041-798-3(pbk.)
1. Owls — Juvenile literature. [1. Owls.] I. Lynch, Wayne, 1948- . II. Title. III. Series.
598.9/ 7 [E] 21   2003 CIP

Fitzhenry & Whiteside acknowledges with thanks the Canada Council for the Arts, and the Ontario Arts Council for their support of our publishing program. We acknowledge the financial support of the Government of Canada through the Book Publishing Industry Development Program (BPIDP) for our publishing activities.

ONTARIO ARTS COUNCIL
CONSEIL DES ARTS DE L'ONTARIO

Canada Council   Conseil des Arts
for the Arts   du Canada

Design by Wycliffe Smith Design Inc.
Printed in Hong Kong

BABY OWL

Text by Aubrey Lang
Photography by Wayne Lynch

Fitzhenry & Whiteside

BEFORE YOU BEGIN

Hello Young Reader,

We love to watch and photograph wild animals, especially baby animals. We wrote this book to share with you some of the adventures in the life of a family of owls.

To photograph the owls in this book, we built a platform 25 feet (8 meters) off the ground in a tree near the nest. During the two and a half months we spent watching them, we were always careful not to scare the owls.

We dedicate this book to the owl guardians Bruce and Bonnie Caywood, and to the landowners Steve and Mary Bruketta.

— Aubrey Lang and Wayne Lynch

TABLE OF CONTENTS

Inside a small wooded area on the North American prairie, a male and female owl are hooting to each other. This is the fourth year that the pair has been together. The male owl has found a nest and hopes his mate will like it.

The days are still very cold and there is deep snow in the woods. It's an unusual time to start a family, but these large owls are the only birds tough enough to begin nesting in the middle of winter.

This is the great horned owl, one of the largest and strongest owls in North America. It doesn't really have horns on its head, just tufts of feathers. When it gets excited, angry, or frightened, it can raise or lower its feathers.

While the mother owl sits on the eggs, the male hides in a nearby tree and guards the woods against other owls.

The male owl does all the hunting in the family. The great horned owl is a perch-and-pounce hunter. He sits in a tall tree or on top of a telephone pole, watching and listening. When an unlucky rabbit, squirrel, or grouse appears, the hungry owl swoops down on silent wings and grabs the animal by surprise. Nothing can escape from his deadly claws, called talons.

For a month the mother owl sits on the nest, day and night. She warms her eggs with the bare skin on her belly. When the father brings food, the mother owl leaves the nest for only a few minutes so she can eat, stretch, and clean and shake her feathers. If the male brings her more food than she can finish in one meal, the female will store the leftovers on the edge of the nest.

The owl chicks hatch three days apart. The biggest owlet hatched first and the smallest one hatched last. When food is scarce, the biggest chick hogs all the food while the smaller ones go hungry. Today, however, there is plenty to eat.

The owlets' eyes open when they are ten days old. That's when they see their mother for the first time.

Life in the nest is pretty boring. Snooze and yawn, yawn and snooze…day after day. But once they are awake, the chicks look up, down, and all around. They are curious about everything. When a woodpecker flies into a nearby tree, the owlets can't stop staring. Even an old feather floating to the ground excites them.

With a steady diet of ground squirrels and pocket gophers, the chicks are growing quickly. The nest is getting crowded. Egg number four never hatched, and it gets kicked out of the nest by one of the active chicks.

At four weeks the young owlets have a new set of fluffy down feathers. They no longer need their mother to keep them warm when the weather is cold or rainy.

The nest is now so crowded, the mother prefers to perch on a branch nearby. She's happy to take a break from nagging chicks that wiggle and squirm, and constantly beg for food. She also has the nasty job of keeping the nest clean and eating any droppings she finds.

When she hops down on the nest to preen the young, the oldest owlet preens her in return.

The nest is a small place for three chubby chicks. Many times a day the owlets stretch and flap their growing wings. They nibble on branches to sharpen their beaks. To exercise their legs, they hop and stretch as tall as they can. One day soon they will be ready to fly and hunt.

The biggest chick is now six weeks old, and brave enough to leave his two younger sisters. He hops to a large branch below the nest. He is wobbly and scared. The owlet almost falls off, but he grips the branch with his sharp talons and flaps his wings to keep his balance. Slowly he climbs the branch until he finds a spot where he feels safe.

A few days later the spunky little owl flaps and glides to the forest floor for the first time. He crashes to the ground in a heap of ruffled feathers. He isn't hurt. He climbs a nearby fallen tree, but it's not high enough for him to feel safe. He waddles over to a better tree, and climbs again.

Even though it's spring, one night a heavy snowstorm catches the family by surprise. By now, all the owlets have left the nest. Each is alone on a perch, close to the ground where it is not as windy and cold. The hungry chicks whistle so their parents can easily find them.

All day long the owlets scream and beg for food. Although they are each as big as a football, they are still helpless.

The forest floor can be a dangerous place for a baby owl. Hungry foxes and coyotes hunt throughout the woods.

A mule deer spots one of the owlets on the ground and walks over for a closer look. The frightened owlet, unaware that the deer is just curious, fluffs up his feathers to make himself look as big as he can. He hisses and snaps his beak. The deer walks away.

By three months of age the chicks are good flyers, but they still can't feed themselves. Even though they can catch insects in the grass, that's not enough. It's much harder to catch squirrels, mice, and birds. The young owls often miss their target.

The parents continue to hunt for their young until the end of summer. Then the owlets will leave home at last, and fly away.

DID YOU KNOW?

- The great horned owl is mainly a nocturnal, or nighttime, hunter. Its large, yellow eyes are adapted for night vision. When hungry, however, the owl will also hunt during the day.

- The owl is a bold and powerful hunter. As well as voles, mice, muskrats, rabbits, ducks, coots, and crows, it will also tackle house cats, skunks, and even porcupines. One unlucky owl, found by a researcher, had 84 porcupine quills embedded in its face, sides, and legs.

- Great horned owls live throughout North America. They occupy a greater variety of habitats than any other owl on the continent. They live in cypress swamps, coniferous forests, deciduous forests, prairies, mountains, and even deserts.

- Like all owls, great horned owls never build their own nests. Commonly they use the old stick nests of hawks, ravens, and crows. They will also nest in tree cavities, on cliffs, and in deserted buildings.

- The eyes of a newly-hatched owlet are blue-gray in color. They gradually change to pale yellow, and finally bright yellow by one month of age.

- Like all owls, the great horned owl regurgitates, or vomits up, pellets of indigestible hair, feathers, bones, teeth, claws, and insects' parts 3 to12 hours after they have eaten. The pellet of a great horned owl may be 5 inches (13 cm) long and shaped like a stubby cigar.

- A pair of great horned owls may stay together and defend the same territory for life. The owls may live for more than 20 years.

INDEX

BIOGRAPHIES

When Dr. Wayne Lynch met Aubrey Lang, he was an emergency doctor and she was a pediatric nurse. Five years after they were married, they left their jobs in medicine to work together as writers and wildlife photographers. For almost twenty-five years they have explored the great wilderness areas of the world — tropical rainforests, remote islands in the Arctic and Antarctic, deserts, mountains, and African grasslands.

Dr. Lynch is a popular guest lecturer and an award-winning science writer.

He is the author of almost twenty titles for adults and children. He is also a Fellow of the internationally recognized Explorers Club, and an elected Fellow of the prestigious Arctic Institute of North America.

Ms. Lang is the author of eleven nature books for children. She loves to share her wildlife experiences with young readers, and has more stories to tell in the Nature Baby Series.

The couple's impressive photo credits include thousands of images published in over two dozen countries.